DELIA BOOKS

Delia Books are designed to teach children about financial literacy.

COPYRIGHT: 2023 DELIA WILLIAMS CURTIS
ALL RIGHTS RESERVED.

ISBN: 9798863730318
PUBLISHED BY DELIA WILLIAMS CURTIS
COVERED DESIGN: DELIA WILLIAMS CURTIS

PRINTED IN THE UNITED STATES OF AMERICA
ALL RIGHTS RESERVED UNDER INTERNATIONAL

COPYRIGHT LAW.
CONTENTS AND/OR COVER MAY NOT BE REPRODUCED IN WHOLE OR IN PART IN ANY FORM WITHOUT THE EXPRESS WRITTEN CONSENT OF THE PUBLISHER.

Dedication

This book is dedicated to my brother, Mondrail.

WHAT IS REAL ESTATE?

By: Delia Williams-Curtis

Real estate is considered as real property. Some types of real estate are industrial, commercial, residential, special use, or raw land. Real estate can be owned by an individual, business, or a trust. Just like choosing a place to live in a video game, real estate is all about finding the perfect spot for different kinds of buildings in the real world.

When people buy or rent houses, they're doing real estate, and sometimes they even become neighbors! Real estate is like a giant puzzle made of houses, apartments, and buildings. There are different types of real estate. People buy and sell these pieces to have a place to live or work.

Purchasing real estate is a huge step to take in your life. The prices of real estate may depend upon the location of the property, size, or type of property. Purchasing real estate can offer steady income, diverse investment portfolio, and capital appreciation.

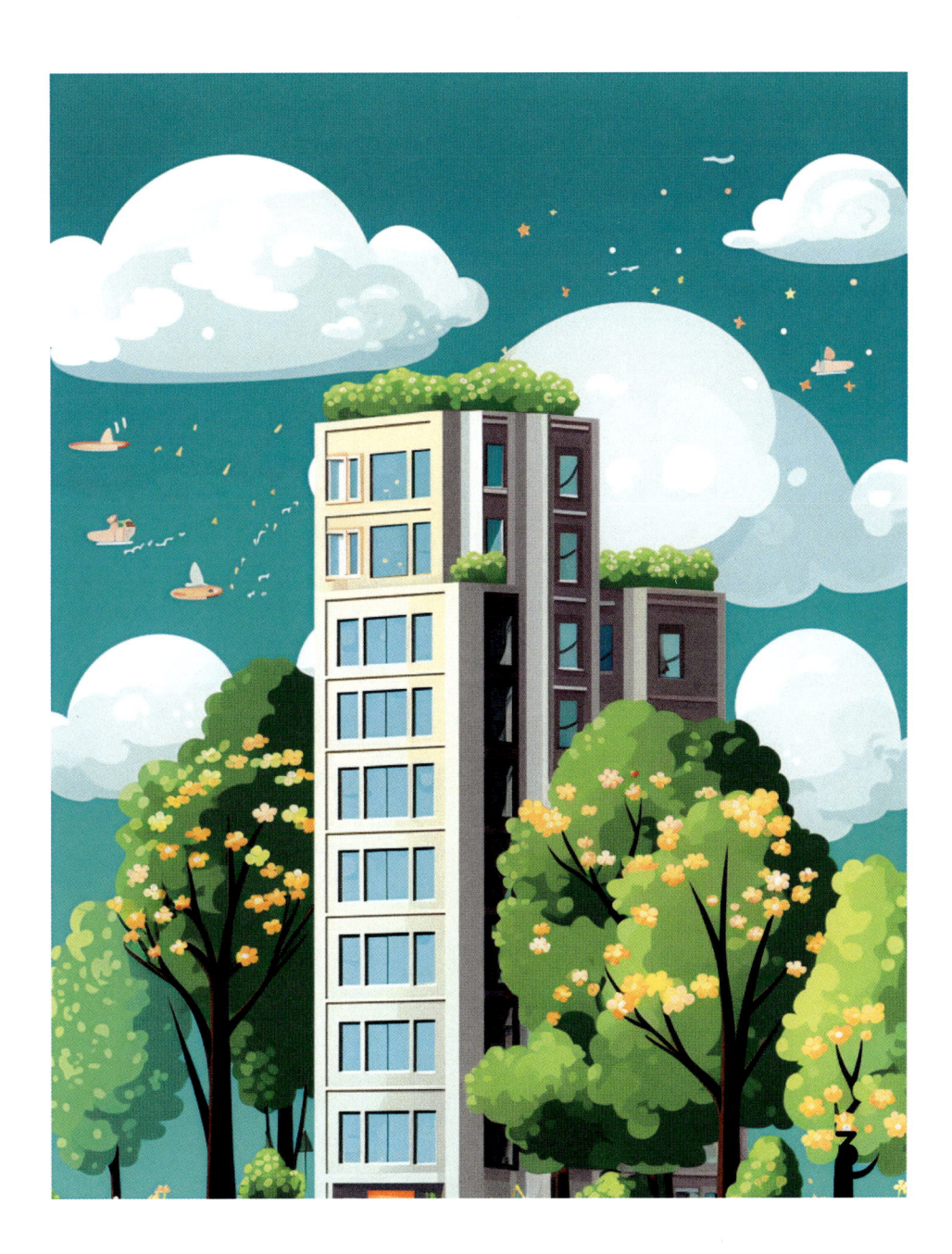

People may considered the size, location, and features like gardens, yards, or swimming pools. Features are essential in real estate because they greatly influence the suitability and value of a property. For example, a swimming pool can make a house more enjoyable, while a spacious kitchen can be important for people who love to cook.

Real estate can be an exciting adventure, like a treasure hunt. Imagine discovering a hidden gem, a house that feels just right. Land, a type of real estate that is the solid ground beneath our feet on which the world is built. It provides a foundation for homes, cities, and natural landscapes. Land comes in all shapes and sizes.

Land real estate includes various categories, including vacant land, agricultural land, or undeveloped properties. Land can be developed or undeveloped. Land that is undeveloped is also called raw land. This type of land sometimes is found in rural areas and is without driveways, public utilities, or buildings. Develop land is prepared for building to take place. You may see develop land in a community.

Individuals can utilize undeveloped land for farming, storage, or recreational activities. Undeveloped land is similar to an empty canvas, offering numerous possibilities. Some individuals choose to cultivate gardens or construct homes, while others prefer leaving it as a natural sanctuary for birds, wildlife, and outdoor adventures, allowing them to use their imagination and create exciting experiences.

Agricultural land is a piece of Earth where farmers work hard to grow crops and take care of animals. It's like a green treasure where nature and farming come together to provide us with yummy fruits, vegetables, and more!

Learning about agricultural land in real estate is important because it helps them see how land can be used for different purposes. Real estate isn't only about houses and stores but also about farms where delicious food grows.

Commercial real estate is not meant for residential living. Within the realm of commercial real estate, various categories exist, including retail, multifamily, industrial, and office space, each catering to different types of business activities and operations.

Investing in commercial real estate can be a smart financial choice as it can generate rental income and potentially appreciate in value over time. The commercial real estate market is a diverse sector and can be influenced by economic trends, location, and the specific needs of businesses.

Warehouses, part of commercial real estate are large commercial buildings, designed for the storage and distribution of goods. They often have high ceilings and extensive shelving or racking systems to maximize storage capacity. Warehouses play a crucial role in the supply chain, ensuring that products are efficiently stored and transported to meet consumer demand.

Retail spaces are commercial properties where businesses sell products or services directly to consumers. These spaces can vary widely, from small boutique shops to large shopping malls. Retail spaces are strategically located in high-traffic areas to attract customers and create a shopping experience that meets their needs and preferences. They often feature storefronts, display areas, and customer-friendly layouts to enhance the shopping experience.

Restaurants, office building, warehouses, residential duplexes are considered as commercial real estate and places that offers workspaces for people. These places are used for people to generate income by leasing the spaces out for business owners. It's where entrepreneurs and companies conduct their operations.

Another type of real estate is residential. This type of property is used for residential purposes. You can see various types of single-family homes in communities throughout cities or towns in the America. Single family homes can vary in the square footage of the home, how many bedrooms, or bathrooms. There are some single-family homes that has large backyards while some have small ones.

A person can invest in real estate by having a rental property, house flipping, or by purchasing a real estate investment trust (REIT). A REIT is a way a person can purchase real estate without physically owning an asset. A person can purchase publicly traded REIT's on a stock market exchange. A REIT can include a diverse portfolio of properties within its holdings.

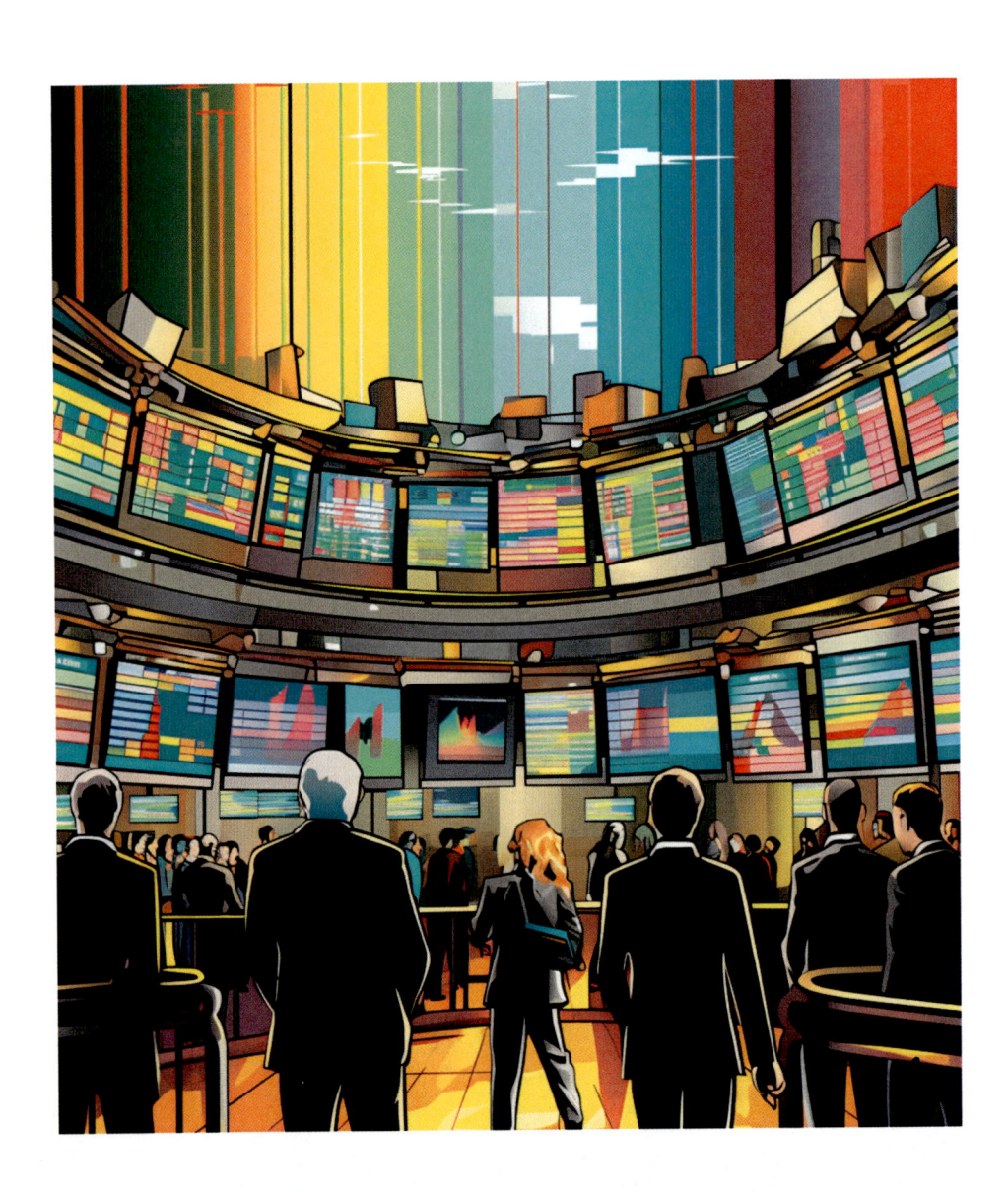

REITs come in various forms, representing a diverse range of real estate sectors, such as hotels, medical facilities, office buildings, malls, warehouses, cell towers, apartment buildings, and retail centers. Investing in a REIT is as straightforward as buying stocks through a brokerage account, providing individuals with easy access to the real estate market without directly owning physical properties.

Special use is another type of real estate category. A special purpose property is purposefully designed to fulfill specific business needs. These properties accommodate a wide range of unique business operations. Special purpose properties are buildings that are made specifically for one particular job or business. They have special features, designs, and equipment that are perfect for that specific use.

Special use properties in real estate are like train stations made just for trains, like railroads! They are designed with everything trains need to run smoothly, like tracks and stations. But because they're made for trains, they can't be used for other things like cars or buses. Some other examples of special use properties are sports arenas, landfills, college dormitories, cemeteries, golf courses, gas stations, hospitals, hotels, or storage units.

A amusement park is a special use real estate property as well. This designed exclusively for kids, featuring a range of thrilling rides and games to create memorable experiences for young visitors. Special use properties play a crucial role in our communities by serving their specific functions efficiently. These properties have features and layouts that match their intended use perfectly.

A college dormitory is a type of special use real estate property where students live while they attend college. These buildings are designed with features like rooms, common areas, and sometimes even dining halls to create a comfortable and convenient place for students to live and study while they pursue their education.

In the real estate process, you start by searching for the perfect property that suits your needs. Next, you make an offer to buy it, and if you can't pay for it all at once, you can get a mortgage, which is a special kind of loan. Once all the paperwork is completed, you can move in and enjoy your new piece of real estate, making it your very own.

A mortgage officer is like a helpful guide in the real estate adventure! They talk to families to figure out how much money they can borrow to buy a house. Then, they help families fill out special papers to make it all official. They work with the bank to make sure everything goes smoothly so everyone can have a happy home!

Banks are like helpers in the real estate adventure! They can lend people money to buy houses or buildings. When someone finds the perfect place and doesn't have all the money, the bank can help them make their dream come true. Then, people pay the bank back over time, like a big piggy bank, so more families can find their special homes too.

A real estate agent someone who helps young individuals and their families find suitable homes or properties that cater to their specific needs and preferences, such as proximity to schools, parks, and child-friendly neighborhoods. They ensure that the housing choices take into account the well-being and comfort of the children, making the transition to a new living space as smooth as possible.

The purchase and selling of real estate play an important factor in our economy. Single family homes are like cozy castles where families live and create wonderful memories together. They usually have a front yard and a backyard, perfect for playing games or having a picnic with friends.

These homes often have bedrooms for every family member, a kitchen for yummy meals, and a living room for family movie nights. They are special because they give families a place to call their very own and share love and laughter.

Investing in real estate can be a wise decision as it provides a stable, long-term asset that can appreciate over time. Additionally, properties situated in family-friendly neighborhoods with good schools and recreational facilities can offer a secure and nurturing environment for children to grow and thrive, making it an ideal choice for parents planning for their family's future.

Real estate can be a special legacy for families that gets passed down through generations. When someone owns a piece of real estate, like a house or land, they can decide to give it to their children or grandchildren as they get older. This often happens when the owner writes something called a "will," which is like a special letter that says who should have the property after they're not here anymore. This way, the property becomes a part of the family's history and can be cherished by many generations to come.

Whether someone wishes to acquire land, invest in REITs, or purchase a single family home, it represents a significant asset and a remarkable achievement. The buying and selling of real estate play a crucial role in our economy, driving growth and contributing to financial stability. It helps people find jobs, like builders, architects, and real estate agents. Plus, it gives money to our towns and states for schools and roads.

About me

Delia Williams Curtis, holds an M.S. degree, is a wife, mom, author and investor. She established Delia Books as a valuable tool to educate children about financial literacy.

Delia has been a teacher on various platforms, sharing her knowledge on topics related to financial literacy and investments.

Delia Books offers a subscription service centered around financial literacy for children aged 7-13. This unique service provides financial education in a convenient package and was born after Delia authored more than 18 books and over 10 journals.

Among her authored works are notable titles such as "The Adventures of Zechariah and the Talking Money Machine," the "Making Sense out of Nonsense for Teens Series," "Investing in the Stock Market for Broke Folks," and the "Stock Sista's Invest like a Boss" journals, all aimed at promoting financial literacy. Originally from Fayetteville, NC, Delia currently resides in Charlotte, NC, with her husband and children.